THE
KINDNESS
COACH

A Pocket Coach

THE
KINDNESS
COACH

DR SARAH JANE ARNOLD

Michael O'Mara Books Limited

First published in Great Britain in 2018 by
Michael O'Mara Books Limited
9 Lion Yard
Tremadoc Road
London SW4 7NQ

A CIP catalogue record for this book is
available from the British Library.

Papers used by Michael O'Mara Books Limited are natural,
recyclable products made from wood grown in sustainable
forests. The manufacturing processes conform to the
environmental regulations of the country of origin.

ISBN: 978-1-78243-918-9 in hardback print format
ISBN: 978-1-78929-015-8 in ebook format

1 2 3 4 5 6 7 8 9 10

www.mombooks.com
Follow us on Twitter @OMaraBooks

Cover design by Ana Bjezancevic
Typeset by Amy Lightfoot

Printed and bound in China

To my parents,

with love and much thought

CONTENTS

'Begin where you are and
such as you are …
and with kindness aforethought,
go about doing good.'

HENRY DAVID THOREAU

INTRODUCTION

Kindness can be defined as a characteristic, a personal value and an ethical way of being that influences how we think, feel and behave towards ourselves, others and the world.

When kindness manifests in our thoughts, it involves consideration, concern, thoughtfulness, understanding, empathy, validation, acceptance and non-judgement. We can recognize kindness in ourselves and others. When kindness manifests in our actions, it encompasses being fair, respectful, considerate, supportive, welcoming, gentle, encouraging, willing to help others and **prosocial** (voluntarily doing something that benefits somebody else). We can enact kind behaviours in daily life.

When kindness manifests in our feelings, there's a felt-sense of care, compassion, warm-heartedness, empathy and sympathy. We feel motivated to be kind and take action.

Kindness, by its very nature, is intrinsically linked with other values that are important for our well-being, such as awareness, assertiveness, self-care, self-respect, gratitude, love, trust, mindfulness, connection, responsibility, friendliness, altruism and generosity. It is influenced by our upbringing, life experiences, present situation, social context and perception. Kindness can be offered with the intention to alleviate suffering or as a general way of being that promotes pleasant feelings, such as happiness, thankfulness, calm and love. There is an appreciation of one another, a sense of unity and mutual support.

What creates kindness?

Philosophers, psychologists, religious scholars and scientists from different schools of thought have debated – and sought to define – the 'fundamental nature' of humans for many, many years. Some people believe that we're innately self-serving, selfish and not altruistic. Some believe that we're neither selfish nor altruistic innately, but that society and our experiences shape us. That is, we're 'conditioned' to be kind or unkind, and our behaviours are reinforced – one way or the other. Others believe that we are innately kind, and we're 'hard-wired' to act in ways that express this. *What do you think?* Scientific psychological research and lived experience offers us some important insights.

Broadly speaking, kindness is an innate capacity that needs to be developed. Caring, compassionate role models in early life are key. They serve as a good example, which teaches us what it means to be kind and unkind. Psychological research confirms that parents, care-givers and teachers play a crucial role in helping us to form bonds, learn empathy, establish caring norms and values, and behave in moral, prosocial ways. Through observing acts of kindness, and through how we're treated by others, we come to learn how to apply kindness to ourselves, how to be kind in our relationships and social interactions and how to extend kindness out to the world.

If we're treated well by others, we come to learn that we're worth being kind to, we believe that others are innately good and that the world deserves our care.

If we've been treated poorly by others (victimized, bullied or abused), it can be much harder to believe that we deserve kindness, that people can be kind and that the world is precious. It can be seen as a hostile, unforgiving and scary place, and people can feel very hurt, afraid and angry.

Time and time again, psychological research highlights that poor parent-child relationships, modelling of unkind or antisocial behaviour (from parents, care-givers, peers, media, society, etc.), a lack of compassion and a lack of appropriate guidance can have a negative impact on a child's ability to develop kind behaviours. As we grow, past pain, abuse of our personal boundaries, difficult emotions and thoughts in the present, stressors, challenging roles and responsibilities, etc., can all contribute to us being unkind to ourselves and others. We might not know how to be with – and helpfully respond to – others' vulnerabilities, and our own.

Knowing how to manage our own stress and pain is crucial if we want to be kind. Fortunately, with time and positive experiences, in which safety and kindness are felt and shared, we can change, heal, learn and grow together.

Whilst there are, undeniably, people who have become self-interested, non-caring, cruel, selfish and competitive – with no wish to change – there's always a reason for this. What's more, it's important to remember that there are many other people in this world who are profoundly kind. Holding on to this fact is essential for our well-being – particularly when we've been hurt by others. Research confirms that humans have a vast capacity for prosocial, cooperative and altruistic behaviours, and instinctual tendencies towards kindness, generosity, self-sacrifice and reverence. These ways of being are vital for the smooth functioning of social groups, our survival and evolution.

What are the benefits of kindness?

Kindness is a virtue that can be very adaptive, i.e., it helps us to survive and thrive as individuals, and as a species. Acts of kindness, both large and small, tend to evoke affirmative, enjoyable feelings within us and others. This is a naturally **reinforcing** experience (it makes us want to keep doing it), because we like to feel good, capable, liked, appreciated and cared for. Relatedly, when we're kind towards others, others tend to be more inclined to be kind to us. Whilst this outcome isn't the intention it is a pleasant, naturally desirable by-product.

Psychological research confirms that acts of kindness benefit our emotional well-being and physical health. For instance, one study (2015) found that people who performed random acts of kindness for four weeks experienced a reduction in their social anxiety. It's possible that these acts of kindness helped people to form more positive perceptions and expectations of others, thereby reducing their anxiety. In another study (2016), participants with high blood pressure were randomly assigned to spend money on others or themselves for three consecutive weeks. Those who spent money on others exhibited a significant decrease in their blood pressure over the course of the study. The positive effect was comparable to that of exercise or medication! The researchers suggest that prosocial spending (on others) can have a positive impact on our heart's health.

Kindness, in its many forms, can positively impact upon our well-being and the well-being of others. It increases feelings of happiness, offers distraction from our troubles, brings life a sense of meaning, improves our self-worth and affords us a sense of community. Reciprocally, it has a positive impact on others' sense of security, physical safety and emotional well-being, too. Kindness has been found to be the most important predictor of satisfaction and stability in all kinds of relationships.

◆ YOUR VALUES ◆

Take a look at this list of common human values and make a note of those that feel very important to you at the moment:

◆ Friendship ◆

◆ Reliability ◆

16

INTRODUCTION

◆ Respect ◆

◆ Forgiveness ◆

◆ Fun ◆

◆ Control ◆

◆ Beauty ◆

◆ Friendliness ◆

◆ Authenticity ◆

◆ Bravery ◆

◆ Acceptance ◆

◆ Activity ◆

◆ Freedom ◆

◆ Reciprocity ◆

◆ Adaptability ◆

◆ Patience ◆

◆ Personal growth ◆

◆ Self Respect ◆

◆ Adventure ◆

◆ Assertiveness ◆

◆ Community ◆

◆ Connection ◆

◆ Autonomy ◆

◆ Caring ◆

◆ Charity ◆

◆ Determination ◆

INTRODUCTION

◆ Dependability ◆

◆ Contribution ◆

◆ Discipline ◆

◆ Gratitude ◆

◆ Excitement ◆

◆ Fairness ◆

◆ Challenge ◆

◆ Commitment ◆

◆ Fitness ◆

◆ Cooperation ◆

◆ Creativity ◆

◆ Willpower ◆

◆ Wisdom ◆

◆ Self-compassion ◆

◆ Compassion ◆

◆ Curiosity ◆

◆ Generosity ◆

◆ Hard work ◆

◆ Empathy ◆

◆ Encouragement ◆

◆ Honesty ◆

◆ Self-care ◆

◆ Loyalty ◆

◆ Self-respect ◆

◆ Effectiveness ◆

◆ Equality ◆

◆ Love ◆

◆ Order ◆

◆ Openness ◆

◆ Humility ◆

◆ Humour ◆

◆ Intimacy ◆

◆ Justice ◆

◆ Kindness ◆

◆ Sensuality ◆

◆ Romance ◆

◆ Sexuality ◆

◆ Knowledge ◆

◆ Learning ◆

◆ Skillfulness ◆

◆ Supportiveness ◆

◆ Listening ◆

◆ Meaningful work ◆

◆ Mindfulness ◆

◆ Non-judgement ◆

◆ Open-mindedness ◆

◆ Safety ◆

◆ Security ◆

◆ Pleasure ◆

◆ Proactivity ◆

◆ Quiet time ◆

◆ Responsibility ◆

◆ Spirituality ◆

◆ Stability ◆

◆ Trust ◆

◆ Rest and relaxation ◆

Awareness of our values can help us to become more kind. We know what we stand for, how we want to behave and how we don't want to be; we know how we want to treat ourselves, others and the world, and we can commit to practising this. Psychological research confirms that when we live a life that's guided by our values, it enhances our well-being and protects us from difficulties like problematic anxiety and depression.

▼ ▼ ▼

Reflect with compassion

◄ What acts of kindness do you offer yourself? ►

◄ What do you do in your daily life that is kind for others? ►

◄ What acts of kindness do you do for the world around you? ►

Now, take a few moments to reflect upon these questions, and write down your answers in a notebook. Self-reflection is a powerful tool. It facilitates self-insight, helps us to understand why we are the way we are, supports us to notice the impact that we have – or can have – on others and ourselves, and enables positive change. It allows us to notice what we like and dislike so that we can be the kind of person that we want to be.

After this period of self-observation, you may realize that you're kind sometimes – in certain contexts – but not in others. Perhaps you notice that kindness is something that you deeply value, but it is not really reflected in your way of being at the moment. Whatever you've noticed, pause now and praise yourself for recognizing it. If you've realized that you're not currently being as kind as you would like to be, then take this moment and begin now. See if you can accept yourself, just as you are, and offer yourself your care and compassion. Acceptance does not mean liking or passive submission. You're simply acknowledging a facet of your reality in this moment. All of us can pick up and develop behavioural habits and ways of thinking that don't fit with our values. Acknowledge your journey so far and recognize that kindness matters to you. You're demonstrating your commitment to learning more about kindness right now, with each word that you read.

The Kindness Coach is for people who are curious about kindness, see it as important, and want their values to determine who they are and how they behave in life. It is my hope that this guide will deepen your understanding of what kindness means to you, enable you to identify when and how you might like to be more kind, and support you to enhance your kindness towards yourself, others and the world.

With warm wishes,

Dr Sarah J. Arnold

▲▲▲

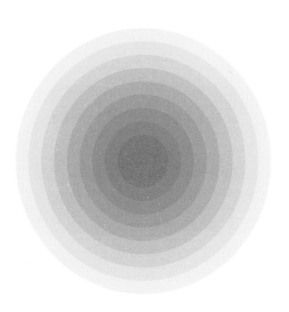

RESPONDING
to yourself
WITH KINDNESS

'Our task is not to seek for love,
but merely to seek and find all
the barriers within yourself
that you have built against it.'

RUMI

RESPONDING
to yourself
WITH KINDNESS

The ability to be kind to yourself – both in daily life and in times of stress and distress – is really important. It means that you can think about, and respond to, yourself in a way that is caring, compassionate, respectful, warm and non-judgemental, rather than critical and condemning.

Regular self-criticism has a detrimental impact upon people's sense of self and well-being in daily life. Research highlights that it's associated with many psychological difficulties, including borderline personality disorder, social anxiety, eating disorders and depression – and that it contributes (significantly) to perpetuating these difficulties. Self-kindness, by contrast, is associated with self-acceptance, emotional well-being and better physical health. It helps us to understand our common humanity, cope well with problems, form healthy, interpersonal relationships, forgive ourselves and believe that we really are 'good enough'.

Like learning to talk or read, self-kindness and self-acceptance come through regular practice; daily, if possible.

ASSERTIVENESS AS SELF-KINDNESS

In order to be kind to ourselves, we need to understand our own worth – believe that we deserve kindness, and know how to extend this to ourselves. We need to know what our rights are, and we need to know how to defend ourselves respectfully when others are unkind to us. These are key features of assertiveness and fundamental principles of self-kindness. Assertiveness is a way of thinking, being – and communicating (more on this in a later chapter) – that facilitates self-kindness. It enables us to express what we think, feel and need in a way that acknowledges and respects our own rights – and the rights of others.

Here are some of the core principles (or beliefs) that underpin what it means to be assertive. When we truly come to believe them, they can help us to be more kind to ourselves as well as others:

- **I am allowed to feel my feelings.**

- **I am allowed to respectfully express my opinions and beliefs if I want to.**

- **I have the right to be listened to.**

- **My thoughts and feelings matter, even if you don't agree with them.**

- **I am allowed to change my mind.**

- **I am allowed to say that 'I don't understand'.**

- I am allowed to make mistakes, and I can learn to own them when they happen.

- I can choose to say yes, and no, for myself.

- I can choose my own priorities.

- I can set my own boundaries, according to what feels comfortable for me.

- I can choose to behave in a manner that I respect, and that respects the rights of others.

- I am allowed to walk away from situations and people that harm my well-being.

Assertiveness, like kindness, is an innate capacity that needs to be developed. Some of us will have been supported to develop assertiveness skills in our younger years, with help and guidance from parents, teachers or friends. Some of us haven't had these kinds of role models, therefore may not be too familiar with these skills. We might not know how to be assertive; we may have learned how to be unassertive (for instance, **passive** or **aggressive** or **passive-aggressive**) in order to cope and get our needs met. Many people fear that being assertive will come across as unkind, therefore they choose to remain passive instead. Unfortunately, this way of being can create resentment, make us inauthentic and actually contribute to us being unkind.

Assertiveness, by its very nature, is a form of honesty that's authentic, kind, respectful and straightforward. If someone is being demanding, rude or unkind, then they're NOT being assertive. Fortunately, assertiveness is a skill that can be taught, learned and mastered at any time in your life.

If you're interested to learn more about what it means to be assertive, check out page 123. You'll find a link to an excellent, free, assertiveness training resource that you can download and use when you choose.

Learning how to be assertive is a form of self-care. People commonly report that knowing how to be more assertive through practice, boosts their confidence, improves their self-esteem, reduces the frequency of challenging emotions and difficult thoughts, and makes them less likely to avoid difficult situations. They come to believe that they can cope well with difficult situations, and that they're worthy of receiving kindness.

◆ SELF-TALK ◆

Thoughts are 'mental events' that enable us to make sense of ourselves, others and the world around us. They allow us to gain knowledge, make decisions, function in our daily lives and thrive. The thoughts that we have about ourselves – and how we speak to ourselves – is called our 'self-talk'. These thoughts tend to be relatively automatic; that is, they pop into our minds unintentionally and outside of our control. Our self-talk reflects the relationship that we've formed with ourselves, as a consequence of the experiences that we've had with others – and our perception of these events. It's shaped by our view of ourselves and events in the present, too. When we listen to our self-talk, believe it and react to it (which we often do), it's called **fusion**. We get drawn into the story that our thoughts are telling us – about us – and it affects us. Sometimes deeply.

Your self-talk might be quite compassionate, generally speaking; it might be very self-critical; it may be largely pessimistic. Tune into your self-talk over the next week and notice how you speak to yourself within the privacy of your own mind. How often do you chastise or unhelpfully criticize yourself? How do you talk to yourself in challenging times? Do you praise yourself for the things you do well? Do you encourage yourself, and offer compassion when you're suffering?

Some of us are very aware of our self-talk; others need to pause, reflect and consider this facet of ourselves. If you have recognized that you would like to be a little kinder to yourself, there are options to achieve this. It *can* be done!

Avoid avoidance

Some of us try to avoid our self-talk, because it can feel threatening. When we believe it, our self-talk can trigger challenging emotions, physical sensations, more thoughts and reactive behaviours that might not help us. Such avoidance is completely understandable; the urge to avoid discomfort (which is an early indicator of possible pain) is hard-wired into us. Unfortunately, avoidance tends to make things worse. By avoiding our self-talk, we're giving ourselves the message that these thoughts are 'bad' and to be feared. What's more, as anyone who has tried this will know, we can't run away from our self-talk for very long. We can distract ourselves from it, we try and avoid it but we cannot escape it. It reflects the relationship that we've formed with ourselves and how we've come to view things – and this has happened for good reason.

So, what can we do when we experience unkind self-talk that doesn't feel very helpful? The automatic thoughts will come to mind whether or not we like them. They're outside of our control. Fortunately, what we *can* control is how we respond to our automatic self-talk. With time and helpful experiences, our self-talk can change. What's more, we can learn a great deal about ourselves and achieve a greater sense of self-awareness – and self-acceptance – when we allow ourselves to really hear our self-talk and try to understand why it is the way that it is.

Noticing your self-talk

The thoughts themselves reflect our fears, past experiences and past pain. First, in response to your self-talk, simply notice it. You can support your mind to do this with phrases such as:

'My mind is telling me ... [insert thoughts].' 'I'm having a thought that ... [insert thought].'

This will help you to remember that your self-talk

consists of thoughts; they may, or may not, be true or helpful. Initially, your aim is to observe your self-talk, with openness, curiosity, compassion and non-judgement. You're aware of your mind thinking thoughts, and you're choosing not to struggle against them. If judgemental thoughts do arise, try to name them for what they are:

'There's a judgemental thought'.

Naming the voice

Self-talk that evokes emotional pain and stress can very easily 'hook us'. We believe it, and we get lost in the story our mind is telling us. For instance, a person who has been bullied for years might criticize themselves a lot and reinforce this story. Try to notice your self-critical voice, and name it when it occurs:

'Ah! There's my self-critical voice again'.

By naming the voice, you can step outside of it – or **defuse** (detach yourself from it) – a little. This can help to lessen its impact because you aren't caught up in the content of your thoughts – you are describing them with some distance. After you've responded to your self-critical voice in this way, you can return your attention back to the present moment and refocus on what matters to you. Alternatively, you can take some time to reflect upon the nature of your self-critical voice, what's contributed to its development, and how you can take care of yourself when it's present.

We can also refer to this voice that calls you names as 'the voice of past pain' – if that's what it's linked to. Alternatively, if it reflects your deeply held fears (of being unlovable, unwanted, incapable or unworthy perhaps) then we can refer to it as 'the voice of fear'. Once again, calling it what it really is helps us to 'un-hook' ourselves from the content of these kinds of thoughts, making it less likely that we'll be swept away in their story.

Does your self-talk help you?

Tune into your self-talk and notice whether or not it helps you. For instance, a person may be at work and struggling with a task and they notice their mind saying: 'I'm never going to be able to do this!' They may begin to feel down, stuck and helpless. Does this self-talk help them? Alternatively, they could take the time to validate how they're feeling, recognizing that they're struggling, and then ask themselves:

'What can I do now, to help myself in this situation? ... I can take a break for five minutes, get some fresh air and then ask my boss for help.'

Notice how this self-talk opens up the possibility of positive change, and a constructive way through a difficult, emotionally demanding situation.

Cultivate compassion

See if you can introduce more compassion into your internal dialogue in response to unkind self-talk. Offer yourself encouragement and support when you can. Speak to yourself gently, as you would to a loved one, with phrases such as:

- You're doing the best that you can.

- You can't be perfect. You don't need to be.

- It's not your fault, or it's not *all* your fault.

- You're human; you will make mistakes sometimes.

- You're allowed to make mistakes; you can consider what you've learned and do things differently next time.

- You have your limitations, and that's okay.

- You're allowed to feel ... [sad; angry; disappointed; anxious; happy; hopeful; proud of yourself, etc.]

- Your feelings are real, important and understandable.

- Your best is good enough.

It takes time, and beneficial experiences, to strengthen new beliefs. Start small, and make sure that you believe the kind things that you say to yourself. Otherwise, it's called 'empty positive thinking' and it isn't very helpful. For example, a person might say to themselves 'you're allowed to make a mistake', but they don't actually believe, deep down, that it's okay. Instead, say something like 'you find it really painful when you make a mistake – it's understandable'. You might not yet be in a place where you believe that you're allowed to make mistakes, but you can compassionately acknowledge your reality at the moment with constructive self-talk like this instead. For support on how to cultivate self-compassion, consult the Helpful Resources section on page 123.

▲▲▲

◆ HOLISTIC SELF-CARE ◆

How we talk to ourselves, respond to our emotions, treat our bodies, address our own needs, what we do and don't do, and our relationships with others all shape us: mind, body and spirit. Many people find it easier to maintain good self-care when life remains more or less on an even keel. However, when we're busy, stressed or distressed, it can be easy to slip into old habits that don't serve our well-being. Here are some habitual ways of being that commonly indicate the need for self-care:

- Skipping meals, over-eating and eating heavily processed fast-food.

- Consuming high-sugar food and drink and/or excessive caffeine and drinking more alcohol.

- Living or working in a messy living space.

- Not making time to see, or speak with, loved-ones.

- Not having quality time alone.

- Working overtime, and/or continuing in a job that you don't like.

- Possessing unrealistic expectations of yourself that fuel your stress.

- Neglecting your personal health and hygiene, such as not brushing your teeth.

- Watching TV or mindlessly surfing the internet.

- Not engaging in any meaningful activities that provide a sense of pleasure or competence.

- Trying to push away, fight with or distract yourself from painful thoughts and feelings (avoidance).

- Harsh or bullying self-talk.

- Not expressing your emotions.

- Avoiding challenging experiences with sleep, drugs, alcohol, and so forth.

- Not getting enough good quality sleep and rest.

If you have done some or all of these things, you're not alone. We all do things sometimes that inhibit us and negatively impact on our well-being. Healthy living is a concept that means different things to different people. However, there's reasonable consensus that a healthy lifestyle is a form of self-kindness that will benefit your well-being, psychologically and physically. It typically involves:

- Keeping active with some form of enjoyable regular exercise and time outdoors.

- Eating good food that's nutritious (free from chemicals, as much as possible).

- Drinking enough water (approximately two litres per day).

- Drinking alcohol safely.

- Spending time with kind, like-minded people; caring for others, too.

- Expressing your feelings.

- Spending quality time alone doing things that you find relaxing, meaningful, personally rewarding and nourishing, such as reading, art or music.

- Doing a job that you enjoy.

- Pursuing activities that you're good at.

- Maintaining good oral hygiene and dental health.

- Maintaining good personal hygiene (taking regular baths/showers).

- Asking for help if you're struggling, and letting others help you.

- Visiting your GP when you have significant concerns about your physical health.

- Learning how to manage stress, cope with your emotions and accept yourself. Seeking psychological support (as required).

- Sleeping well.

- Not smoking and avoiding dangerous drugs and mis-use of prescribed drugs.

What's your mind saying about this list? Take a moment, and notice your thoughts. There's a lot of advice out there about what we *should* be doing; it can feel a bit overwhelming. Most of us know what things are good for us, and what things aren't, yet we get drawn into old ways of being that sabotage us.

See if you can take some time to understand what blocks you from living well and taking care of yourself. The reasons for poor self-care vary for different people at different times. Sometimes we just want to do what we want to do; we feel the need for autonomy and control, and we behave in ways that reflect this. Sometimes we might not know what we need, or we might feel scared to try for our own reasons. Other times, not knowing how to cope with difficult thoughts and feelings can impact on our self-care; from time to time, some of our needs are expressed in a way that impacts upon our self-care. For instance, the need for rest might manifest as procrastination and unwittingly create more stress. If consistent self-care was simple, we'd all be doing it – all of the time. Fortunately, there's lots that we can do to help ourselves.

The first step is to understand why you fall into

certain habitual behaviours. Mindfulness practice (which we'll come to soon), self-monitoring and personal reflection (such as journaling) can help you to make sense of these things independently. What signs might you notice when your self-care is slipping? What can you watch out for? Speaking with a qualified therapist, and talking to friends or family, may also be of help. Try to spot why and when your self-care slips, and learn to recognize those moments of resistance, when you actively turn away from the option of self-care in favour of something self-destructive or less helpful. With this self-awareness, you can befriend yourself with compassion and begin to proactively change old patterns – rather than mindlessly repeating them, and fruitlessly judging yourself. Many people mistakenly frame self-care as a luxury that they can't afford. Please remember that it is not a luxury – nor is it self-indulgent – it's a necessity, and an act of self-preservation for all of us, particularly in challenging times. You deserve this care, too; it's another common block to forget this. With time and commitment, the daily practice of taking care of yourself – physically and emotionally – will become a new way of being. You're in charge of your own life.

✦ BEFRIENDING YOUR EMOTIONS ✦

Learning how to notice your emotions, understanding what they mean, and knowing how to respond to them is a crucial facet of self-kindness. It enables us to acknowledge how and why different experiences impact us; it supports us to know what our needs might be, and it facilitates emotional stability, self-awareness and healthy self-care. The more that you can understand both your heart and mind – and take care of them – the more emotional space you'll have to think about others' needs. It can be very hard to fully engage with others – to share in their joys and support them in their sorrows – if you feel like you are sinking.

Express yourself

Emotional self-expression is crucial for you if you are to maintain and enjoy good mental health. It's an important part of self-care that will help you to understand yourself and feel more emotionally grounded. Writing about your experiences, making art, pottery, dancing, singing, making music (or just noise!) with musical instruments, talking to friends, psychological therapy, etc., are all cathartic ways in which you can do this. It's also important that you allow yourself to cry when you need to. It acknowledges your feelings, helps to communicate your internal experiences to others, and releases and reduces emotional stress.

What do you do that helps you to express how you're feeling? If you notice that you're not doing anything right now, that's okay. It's not too late to start. Trying something unfamiliar can feel a little bit scary and uncomfortable at first, but when you get used to it – and you find the right mode of expression for you – it can be incredibly freeing.

◆ NAVIGATE YOUR EMOTIONS ◆

The NAV technique

Another essential act of self-kindness involves learning how to respond to ourselves in a constructive way, with kindness and compassion, when we're feeling emotionally challenged:

1. **Naming** what we're feeling

2. **Accepting** what we're feeling

3. **Validating** what we're feeling

The acronym 'NAV' (Name, Accept and Validate) can help you to remember this. Try it the next time you notice yourself feeling strong or challenging emotions. With each emotion, see if you can:

1. Name your emotion(s) using one word for each emotion you notice

'I am feeling ... [anxious, sad, frustrated, lonely and confused].'

We have all of our feelings for good reason. Different emotions convey different messages about our thoughts, needs and experiences. When we can identify them – and name them – it helps us to acknowledge and affirm our own experience, and begin to identify our needs. Our emotions tell us important information about our internal and external experiences. They facilitate self-awareness, motivate us, prepare us to take action, enable us to protect ourselves, communicate crucial things to others and evoke others to respond to us. They need to be evocative in order to get our attention.

2. Accept that this exists for you right now

When you're practising acceptance, you are simply acknowledging that your emotions are real, they exist, and you're choosing not to fight against them or run from them (because this causes more suffering to arise). You don't need to like how you're feeling; acceptance doesn't mean liking. When we acknowledge what exists

– without judging our experience – it protects us from escalating our stress reaction. When we struggle with our emotions, we tend to feel emotions about our emotions, e.g., hopelessness about our sadness.

Of course, accepting our emotions isn't easy. It goes against our natural instincts to struggle against unpleasant sensations in order to 'protect' ourselves from possible harm. Remember, these feelings are not trying to hurt you, and they will pass. You can help your mind to understand that your emotions are not dangerous, in spite of how they might feel, every time you consciously accept their presence. Try to breathe with your feelings, and allow them to be here with you – as best you can. We can learn a great deal about who we are, what our needs are, and what we can do to ease our own suffering once we accept how we're feeling.

3. Validate your feelings

When you're practising validation, you are taking

the time to privately reassure yourself that what you're feeling is real and important. All of your feelings exist for good reason – even if you don't understand what's triggered them just yet. You can validate your experience, nonetheless, by reminding yourself that you're human and you are allowed to feel this way.

Challenging emotions are normal and natural, for all of us. They're not a sign of weakness or failure, as society can suggest. Psychological research confirms that naming, accepting and validating these emotions (rather than judging them, and ourselves) reduces their intensity, improves our psychological well-being and protects against mental health difficulties. With regular practice, the NAV technique helps people to tolerate their emotions; it tends to enhance self-awareness, self-compassion and emotional stability, too. It's a way of turning towards our pain with kindness, rather than battling against it with judgement.

Of course, it's not always easy. These are

deceptively difficult skills to master, and different people find different aspects harder than others. For instance, if you've come from a family that didn't tend to acknowledge your emotions, you might find that it takes a while to get used to naming your emotions. What's more, acceptance can be really hard because it goes against our natural instincts to accept pain – every fibre of our being wants to fight it, run from it or freeze in it to make it go away because the brain processes it as a warning sign of potential danger. Simply knowing this can help you to practise these skills with more patience and compassion. It's incredibly valuable once you get the hang of it. Of course, you won't always remember – or feel able – to use it, and that's okay, too. It can be enough to hold the intention to try. Practise when you can, and when you want to!

▲ ▲ ▲

◆ NURTURE ◆

Self-soothing is an important personal skill. It means doing things for ourselves that feel nourishing, soothing and comforting when we're feeling emotionally challenged. The aim isn't to get rid of how we're feeling. The point is to acknowledge our suffering – behave in line with the idea that we don't deserve to suffer more – and do simple things for ourselves that help to improve the moment that we're in. This facilitates self-kindness, a sense of personal autonomy (being able to choose to do things for ourselves) and self-compassion. It can enable us to experience a greater sense of peace, stabilize the mind and soothe emotional distress. Long-term, this way of being can boost our self-worth and protect against difficulties like depression.

What kinds of (helpful) things bring you comfort? How would you treat someone you love who is going through a hard time? How can you respond to yourself with kind-hearted compassion when you need it most? If you don't know just yet, that's okay. It can take a while to figure these things out. Try to think of things that might appeal to your five senses. That is, things you can see, hear, touch, taste and smell.

▼ ▼ ▼

Here are some examples that you might like to try, the next time you're feeling the need for some self-kindness.

Sight: resting with soothing coloured lights; spending time in nature.

Sound: practising a 'loving-kindness' guided meditation; listening to a soothing podcast or audiobook.

Touch: cuddling with a pet; wearing items of clothing that feel comforting.

Taste: the taste of a much-loved drink; chamomile and lavender tea.

Smell: using an aromatherapy burner with soothing essential oils; a particular fragrance

You might notice the urge to 'soothe' yourself in a way that's counter-productive, albeit effective in the short-term. For instance, drinking more alcohol, bingeing on junk-food or shopping. See if you can respond to yourself with kindness – prioritize your well-being – and do things for yourself that truly nurture you instead. You deserve kindness and care, and you can offer this to yourself when you need it.

◆ PERSONAL THERAPY ◆

Personal therapy is for *anyone* who wants to talk about the things that matter to them, in a safe and confidential space, with someone who's professional, supportive and impartial. It's an act of self-kindness to seek and receive therapy. It can benefit our mental health, spiritual health and physical health, too. Psychological difficulties and general life issues can negatively impact upon our ability to behave as we would like, affect our confidence, autonomy, willingness to be sociable, and our ability to be kind to ourselves and others. Many people find that psychological therapy helps them to know themselves better, respond to their difficulties more effectively, live a more fulfilling life and be kinder towards themselves and others. Please note that all therapists are different. It's important that you find a therapist that's right for you.

✦ MINDFULNESS TRAINING ✦

Mindfulness is an ancient Eastern practice, which originates from Buddhist and Hindu philosophies. It's an important aspect of yoga too. It's found its way into mainstream psychology and popular culture in the West relatively recently because mental-health professionals have studied it and realized its remarkable benefits. In essence, mindfulness means: **tuning in to the present moment, fully and intentionally, with an attitude of kindness, compassion, acceptance, non-judgement, openness and curiosity.** It's a way of being that helps us to be more aware of our internal environment (thoughts, feelings, sensations and urges) and our external environment (others and the world around us). It teaches us how to observe and respond to our experiences – reduces suffering and enhances compassion. It supports us to:

- greet challenging thoughts, feelings and sensations with a mindful attitude, and develop trust in our ability to tolerate them

- learn how to treat ourselves with kindness, compassion and acceptance, rather than judgement. It gives us permission to be imperfect and human, as all of us are!

- develop the qualities of openness and

patience, as we learn to let things unfold naturally rather than clinging on to ideas about 'how things *should* be'

- free ourselves from learned patterns of thinking and behaving that no longer serve us; replacing them with more compassionate ways of being.

Like kindness, and assertiveness, mindfulness is an innate capacity that can also be grown. You can learn how to be more mindful through formal meditation training (see page 123). You can also adopt a mindful attitude when you engage in everyday activities, like walking, eating or bathing, which we refer to as **informal mindfulness**. Reliable research confirms that mindfulness practice significantly benefits psychological well-being and physical health. It can:

- help us to cope better with stress and anxiety

- reduce the likelihood of depression relapses

- reduce physical pain, and help us to cope better with pain

- improve immune system functioning

- help us to make better decisions, and sleep better

- support us to know and accept who we are; improve our self-care and self-esteem

- enhance our sense of connectedness with others

- support us to be less reactive and more compassionate, kind and non-judgemental towards ourselves (and others).

Loving-kindness meditation

Loving kindness is a concept in meditation practice, which specifically supports us to develop an attitude of kindness, compassion and acceptance towards ourselves, others and the world that we inhabit together; it's akin to unconditional love. It teaches us how to receive kindness ourselves, and to send out this wish for others and all living beings.

▼ ▼ ▼

To meditate, sit comfortably in a quiet space. Try to embody a sense of dignity and wakefulness in your sitting position. When you're ready, tune into yourself breathing gently, in and out. You are taking this time for yourself, as an act of self-care. Your intention is to cultivate loving kindness within yourself to begin with. When you're familiar with this process, you can allow your eyes to gently close.

Receiving loving kindness

Bring your awareness to yourself – to your body, breath, mind and emotions. With a sense of warmth and genuine care, see if you can truly wish yourself well. Place your hand on your chest, and breathe with these words:

• • • • ●

May I be safe,
and as healthy as I can be.
May I accept myself,
and care for myself with kindness.
May I be free from suffering.

● • • • •

It may be helpful to imagine a person or pet, who loves you or has loved you unconditionally. Bring to mind their love for you, really feel it and allow yourself to receive it. Alternatively, you might acknowledge that you have experienced a lack of love and support in your life. If this is the case, then try and tune into the fact that you deserve kindness too. Breathe gently as you sit with these words and repeat them several times, at your own pace. You might find it hard to believe and accept these words initially; you might notice some resistance in your mind and body, and your mind might wander off. This is completely normal. Observe your thoughts with a mindful attitude, as best you can, and then gently return the focus of your attention back onto these phrases. It's a learning process to hold yourself in your own heart and mind – and truly wish yourself well.

▲▲▲

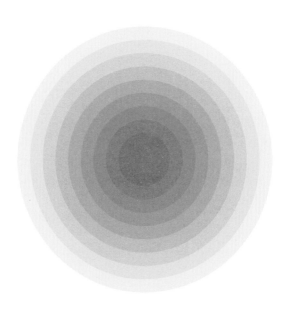

RESPONDING

to others

WITH KINDNESS

'Kindness in words creates
confidence.
Kindness in thinking
creates profoundness.
Kindness in giving creates love.'

LAO TZU

RESPONDING
to others
WITH KINDNESS

Sending out loving kindness to someone you care about

We continue with loving-kindness practice and meditation here. Bring to mind someone that you care about deeply; they might be a close friend, partner, family member or a person who inspires you. Allow yourself to feel grateful for their existence. Visualize them if you can, or say their name to yourself. Feel the warmth of your connection with them, and wish them well by repeating these words:

· · · ● ●

May you be safe,
and as healthy as you can be.
May you accept yourself,
and care for yourself with kindness.
May you be free from suffering.

● ● ● · ·

Observe any thoughts or feelings that arise with a mindful attitude, and then return the focus of your attention back on to this person. Imagine these wishes being received by your loved one; it warms their heart. Notice what this feels like for you, too.

Sending out loving kindness to someone neutral

When you're ready, think of someone that you don't know well – someone you feel neutral about, whom you see in your local community. Hold them in your heart and mind, and wish them well, too – repeating these words:

· · · · ●

May you be safe,
and as healthy as you can be.
May you accept yourself,
and care for yourself with kindness.
May you be free from suffering.

● ● ● ● ·

Let kindness fill you, as you inhale and exhale gently.

Sending out loving kindness to someone you find difficult

Now, if you feel able to do so, think of someone whom you find difficult. Perhaps this person has hurt you. Offer them a seat in your mind, and make room for your feelings, too. See if you can wish them well, as best you can, for they, like you, have felt difficult emotions. They too have faced losses, uncertainty and challenges in life. May they feel cared for, too:

• • • • ●

May they be safe,
and as healthy as they can be.
May they accept themselves,
and care for themselves with kindness.
May they be free from suffering

● • • • •

You can practise wishing them well in their life without necessarily wanting them in yours. You are allowed to find this person difficult. Place your hand on your chest, with kindness and warmth, and return to your breath once more. [Note: please select someone who feels manageable to hold in your mind right now. You can pick someone whom you find even more difficult later on, after some time and practice.]

Sending out loving kindness to everyone

Now see if you can open your heart and extend loving kindness to everyone everywhere – with no discrimination or separation:

· · · ● ●

May we be safe,
and as healthy as we can be.
May we accept ourselves,
and care for ourselves with kindness.
May all of us be free from suffering.

● ● ● · ·

Repeat these words and hold this sentiment as you wish. When you're ready, simply open your eyes.

▲ ▲ ▲

Practising a loving-kindness meditation is one way in which you can set your intention to care for others with kindness. Our relationships with others matter a great deal; our care for them and our ability to appreciate them can promote good mental and physical health, enhance our psychological well-being, meet our basic human needs for intimacy and love, enrich our lives with joy, and add to our sense of purpose and meaning in life.

Of course, one could argue that it's not enough to wish others well in our minds. In order to build, sustain and enjoy long-lasting bonds, and positively affect others' lives, we need to be able to demonstrate our care. The primary way in which we do this is through our communication with others. Here are some key concepts to reflect upon, practise and keep in mind.

KINDNESS IN COMMUNICATION

We are innately social beings, and the communication that we share with one another matters. Verbal and non-verbal communication helps us to convey important information to others about ourselves, our experiences and our needs. Effective communication can create and sustain positive connections with others, facilitate new knowledge, positive change and pleasant emotions, and it can help us to cope effectively when challenging internal or external experiences occur. Kindness in communication gives others the message that they're of value and worthy of attention, because we care enough to listen and truly engage with them. It fosters a sense of unity, combats loneliness, enriches both parties and enables us to learn from each other. There are many different ways in which you can reflect kindness in your communication with others.

Active listening

Active listening involves being physically and emotionally available when you're speaking to someone: demonstrate that you're ready and willing to listen with an open body posture, a warm gaze and facial expressions that reflect your interest; see if you can be fully present during the communication, rather than, for example, half listening whilst scrolling through your phone. Really listen to what is being said and notice *how* it is said. Try not to interrupt the person whilst they're speaking, and let them know that you're following them with verbal responses such as 'I hear you'. Body language, such as silent nodding after certain things have been said, can also be an effective way of conveying your engagement with them. You can demonstrate your curiosity in someone else's experiences, interests, struggles, hopes and dreams by asking questions rooted in genuine interest. Open-ended questions, like 'What happened then?' or 'What was that like?', will invite the person to say more. This will help to deepen your understanding of their experience and facilitate empathy.

Beware of 'story-stealing'

Imagine you're listening to a friend speak about their day, when they mention that they've bought a new book and they're excited to begin it. Naturally, the words 'book' and 'reading' remind you that you've just read a book that you really enjoyed, and the automatic urge to share this occurs. You eagerly begin talking about your reading experience, and recommend that your friend reads it, too. Politely they respond. This in turn diverts the conversation onto another topic, and you never learn what excited your friend about their new book. Later in the conversation you share that your partner upset you this morning because they were short-tempered with you. You wish to talk about this experience with your friend and share your thoughts and feelings about it. You want their advice and some gentle support. Instead, your friend begins to talk about a similar experience that they had recently with their partner. The conversation moves on, and your thoughts, feelings and needs remain unheard and unexplored. This is an example of two people unintentionally 'story-stealing'.

Story-stealing is something that many of us do, and it can be unthinking or well-intended. Nevertheless, it can be very unhelpful, inhibit our ability to be kind, deny us the chance to learn more about someone's inner world, negatively impact upon the quality of our relationships and (correctly or incorrectly) send the message that we aren't genuinely interested in the person that we're talking to.

The urge to story-steal is natural, and very human, but you don't need to act upon it. You can interrupt this automatic process, simply by noticing your thoughts and your urge to speak. You can try to make a mental note of your point, and share it later on in the conversation. Allow the person in front of you to tell their story first, listen intently and offer empathy instead.

Empathy

Empathy is the ability to feel and understand someone else's emotion and experience, as if they were happening to you, without losing your objectivity as the observer. It's a virtue that enables us to trust each other, resolve interpersonal conflicts, support each other, form lasting close relationships, feel a sense of connection, and communicate in a way that promotes honesty, assertiveness and genuine kindness.

Empathy is another innate capability that needs development, and it takes practice. You can learn how to recognize when you're not being empathetic, and you can learn how to become more empathetic with good teaching and a mindful attitude. Some people experience a natural inclination towards being empathic more than others. This is significantly related to our early life experiences, such as how we were parented, our parents' level of empathy, and our ability to reflect upon these experiences and make changes to our own way of being as appropriate. If you'd like to deepen your ability to empathize with others, here are some tips:

1. Really listen to what the other person is saying, and try to understand what's going on for them. When you empathize with someone, you are always empathizing *about* something. For instance, perhaps a situation breached someone's basic needs for food, shelter, clothing, love, friendship, intimacy, autonomy, freedom or belonging. Perhaps their emotional or physical welfare was threatened in some way and they're suffering. Maybe something or someone has infringed

upon their rights, goals, values or desires. In order to empathize, you need to understand what's happened and why the person finds this difficult; you need to get a sense of the facts, their perception and how they're feeling.

2. In order to engage fully with others, we need to 'bracket' (acknowledge and put aside) the things that come to mind as someone else is talking. We need to temporarily suspend our own point of view – our criticisms, opinions and beliefs – in order to enter the internal world of another person. You don't need to agree with their perspective, but you do need to be able to understand the world through their eyes. Focus on what their experience *means* to them, or for them, and how it *feels* for them; you're not focusing on whether or not their perspective is helpful.

3. If you get emotionally triggered and begin reliving your own pain (related to a similar

situation), it will negatively impact upon your ability to empathize because your focus will naturally shift onto yourself. Understanding what's yours and what's theirs, noticing how these things are similar and different, and bracketing what's yours will support you to focus and empathize with them.

4. Use your own experiences as a source of insight to deepen your empathy, but remember that individuals experience similar situations very differently.

5. You can still empathize with someone, even if you haven't gone through the same experience yourself. You might not know what it feels like to be suicidal, for example, but you may know what it's like to feel trapped and hopeless. You can use your experience of these emotions to deepen your empathy and tune into the emotions, needs and values that we all share as human beings.

6. In order to empathize, you need to feel bad for someone and recognize the adversity that they're experiencing or have experienced. You can convey your interest, care and compassion with active listening.

7. You can reflect back and interpret how the other person might be feeling. For example, someone who feels betrayed by their friend might say: 'I just can't believe that she would do this!' You might reply with something like: 'You're really shocked and hurt'. You might also add an additional statement to reflect your empathy, such as 'This has really shattered your trust in her'.

8. You can use words that reflect the fact that you're seeing their feelings as valid (real and important), such as 'understandably' and 'I would feel the same' or 'of course you felt ...'

9. You can empathize with someone – about their experience of something or someone

else – without saying things that fuel anger or resentment within them. Notice yourself getting drawn into toxic dynamics such as malicious gossip, and consider how you might feel if people were saying these things about you; act accordingly.

10. Even if you think that others' emotional reaction is disproportionate to what's happened, try to understand that it will be proportionate to their thoughts. For instance, if someone's beloved partner is late coming home and it's feared that they've been killed in an accident then anxiety would be a natural reaction. You can empathize with their fear, and recognize that you would feel scared, too, if your mind was telling you this.

11. Try your best not to interrupt the person whilst they're speaking.

12. Remember, empathy is different than sympathy. Sympathy means that you feel

sorry for someone's plight, but it doesn't require you to share their perspective or emotions; empathy does.

13. You might notice the urge to give advice or problem-solve for someone when they're stressed or in distress. Even if this is well-intentioned, it can severely interfere with your ability to empathize. Empathize first; problem-solve second.

14. In situations that require empathy, a problem of some kind tends to be highlighted. Try to help others to figure out what they think, feel and need, rather than telling them what they 'should' do. It will facilitate their autonomy, self-esteem and confidence in their ability to make decisions for themselves, which is protective against problematic anxiety and depression.

15. Despite our best intentions – we don't, won't and can't always get it right. Sometimes we will

misunderstand others; we'll get hooked into problem-solving, for our own reasons; we'll invalidate the other person by our reactions or responses and upset them unintentionally; we might feel bored and 'wander off' mentally when someone is trying to share something with us. When these things happen, notice it mindfully and try to understand why it was hard for you to empathize with this person in that moment. Maybe something they said resonated with you deeply and temporarily blinded you to their feelings. Maybe you notice that you're not very empathic with some people due to your past experiences and learned behaviours. Whatever the reason, take your mind back to the idea of self-kindness – notice your self-talk and try to offer yourself compassion and forgiveness. Allow yourself to make mistakes, and reflect upon what you might want to do differently next time. Empathy skills can be built and improved with practice and mindfulness. All that you need is the willingness to learn, and the willingness to try.

Assertive communication

Assertiveness in our communication with others is an act of kindness that really matters. When we're being passive, we're usually thinking a great deal about someone else's needs and neglect to consider our own. When we're being aggressive, we're thinking about our own needs much more than the other person's. When we're being **assertive**, however, we're considering our own needs *and* the needs of others; we're communicating in a kind, considered and emotionally grounded way, which acknowledges and respects our own rights – and others' rights, too.

Being assertive when we communicate gives others the message that we respect them, want to understand them, value them, value our relationship with them and care enough to want to resolve misunderstandings. It creates a sense of safety because we're being transparent and authentic about our perception, needs and experiences. It helps them to feel understood and known because we are listening, empathizing and responding in a constructive way – even if we're upset.

If someone is being hostile, here are things to keep in mind and consider in the moment:

- Take a few mindful breaths, notice and validate your own feelings, and decide how you want to respond in this particular situation.

- Assertiveness can transform an argument into a constructive conversation. If you decide to be assertive, try to remain grounded and see if you can understand why they're being this way. Ask questions sensitively, and give them a chance to explain.

- Assertively highlight that when they ... [for

example, shout at you], you feel ... [upset and angry]. You're highlighting the links between their way of being and your experiences, without blaming or judging them.

- If their anger seems to be about something that you've done, use empathy to understand why it upset them, acknowledge this and apologise sincerely. Mistakes don't mean that you're bad, unworthy, incapable or unlovable; they mean that you're normal, human and have more to learn (like all of us!). The more you can recognize and admit to your mistakes the more you can learn and grow.

Getting lost in self-blame and over-focusing on how bad you feel (because you made a mistake) will limit your ability to empathize with, and be kind to, the other person (because it shifts the focus of your attention from them onto you in an unconstructive way). Forgive yourself; it will benefit your self-esteem and positively impact upon your way of being with the other person.

- You may want to resolve the issue, or come to some sort of shared understanding at least. Sometimes this is possible. Other times, one or both parties need time to understand their own thoughts and feelings, and calm down, before they can address each other with kindness (rather than hostility).

- If the other person is unwilling to explain, or they continue to be rude, accept that they may be dealing with something that isn't your fault, but which explains their mood and behaviour. Humanize them, and take the necessary steps to take care of yourself. Reach out to them again with compassion, if you want to, after some time has passed.

- You can accept someone, and behave respectfully towards them, without liking all parts of them. Don't confuse kindness with passivity, though. You can be kind and considerate of the other person's feelings whilst saying yes and no for yourself, expressing your own needs honestly, and asserting your own boundaries.

When each party says what they think, feel and need, and this is met with kindness, it makes it less likely that resentments will form, fester and damage the bond. Of course, being assertive doesn't guarantee that we'll be heard or get our needs met, but it gives us the best chance. Crucially, it helps us to be kind – even in really difficult situations.

▲ ▲▲

◆ SMALL BUT MIGHTY ◆ ACTS OF KINDNESS

There are many ways and opportunities to be kind. Here are some ideas for you:

- Giving and receiving truthful feedback takes courage and requires kindness. If you need to offer any form of criticism, use 'the feedback sandwich': give an affirmative (positive) observation, a constructive criticism and then another affirmative observation. It can help you to be assertive and develop good bonds, and help the other person to trust others, learn and grow whilst feeling valued and encouraged.

- Use your experience to mentor a colleague or friend and help them to achieve their goal. Be honest about what you can do, in terms of your time and emotional resources.

- Stand up for others who are struggling to defend themselves. Don't standby whilst someone else is being bullied or mistreated. Your support can give someone the message that they're worthy of support and it might help them to believe in themselves or know what to say next time.

Simple kindnesses towards strangers matter. It conveys that some people do care and the world has goodness in it. Think about trying these simple gestures:

- When you get the opportunity, help someone carry their push chair or suitcase up or down stairs.

- Pick up a toy that's been lost by a child and put it somewhere visible to increase the chance of them finding it, or hand it in if there's a lost and found service.

- Tell someone that they've dropped something on public transport and give their item back to them.

- Give up your chair to someone older, disabled, or who simply seems like they might need some kindness.

- If it feels safe, stop and speak to a stranger who's in distress or looking lost. Ask if there's anything that you can do to help them.

- Say a warm hello to people who work on the tills in shops; ask them how they are.

- Buy a drink and some food for a homeless person. If you can afford to do so, consider buying them a pop-up tent.

Take the initiative and offer help clearly. People can find it hard to ask for what they need. Others may decline your help if they don't want it; if this is the case try to respect it.

- If you're out with some friends and you see someone alone who looks like they might wish for company, invite them to join you.

- Let others know that you're thinking of them on difficult days, such as Mother's Day, if their mum has passed away.

- Notice if one of your friends needs a little TLC, and invite them around for a chat and some quality time together.

- When someone goes through a personal crisis, like a bereavement, chronic illness or accident, many people offer their kindness immediately. This is very valuable; a home-cooked meal, a message of support, or an empathic conversation can really help. What many people don't realise is that the need for support and kindness continues after the initial trauma has passed. Long afterwards, people can still be reeling from the effects of a crisis that they've experienced. Invite them to speak about their experiences, and ask them what they need or would like. Let them know that their suffering hasn't gone unrecognized.

- Celebrate others' successes and offer words of encouragement. Mindfully notice any feelings of jealousy and envy, accept them with compassion and try not to judge yourself. Then, do your best to refocus your energy back onto the other person with kindness and genuine interest. Acknowledge that it can feel hard to celebrate and wish them well when you're struggling or not achieving in the same way. Try to reflect upon what you have achieved and what you're currently doing well at.

- Show your gratitude and appreciation for the people that you love and care for: kind words, spontaneously sending them a card in the post, or leaving them a Post-it note with a thoughtful message on it.

Try to give without expectation or the wish to receive. Mindfully notice any expectations that are there.

- Give someone a hug, when you want to. It releases a feel-good chemical called oxytocin, which reduces cardiovascular stress and improves immune-system function. Hug with authenticity, genuine care and kindness; don't hug someone half-heartedly if you're not feeling like it!

- Ask someone how they are, and really listen to their reply. Remember what they've said, and follow up on it in the days to come.

- Offer your sofa or spare room to a friend who temporarily needs a place to stay.

- Share what you know with others. 'Skill swaps' are another great way of learning new things and connecting with others. For example, I could teach someone basic counselling skills and, in return, they could give me drum lessons.

- Be mindful of others and consider their personal space, give others your eye contact and a friendly smile to acknowledge their presence in the world with you.

- Try to be well-mannered and courteous. You never know what someone else is going through.

- Be curious about others' interests, stories, hopes and dreams, and ask questions to reflect this. It combats loneliness, forms bonds, and fosters a sense of unity and shared experience.

Observe and listen to get a sense of what kind of care and kindness others want, need and will respond well to. What might help them to feel cared about? You may not always get this right, but most people will appreciate your effort. The more that you put kindness into practice, the better you will be at responding helpfully to others' needs.

Always check in with yourself, however, and make sure that your own needs are being met, too. Depriving yourself of kindness in order to give to others is not healthy, and often signals that you're avoiding issues and conflicts within yourself. In the long run, this will be exhausting and detrimental to your well-being.

▲ ▲ ▲

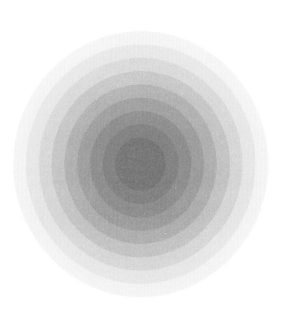

RESPONDING
to the world
WITH KINDNESS

'Kindness begets kindness
evermore.'

SOPHOCLES

RESPONDING
to the world
WITH KINDNESS

In the face of everything that's frightening in the world, during hardship, suffering and strife, kindness offers us an antidote. Let it radiate from you, as you consider not only yourself and others but the world at large, too, and ask:

◄ How can you make a difference to this world, whilst you are here? ►

◄ What kind of person do you want to be, and what do you want to stand for? ►

◄ What do you appreciate about our world? ►

When we're able to extend kindness to all living beings – and the planet – it creates a better world for all of us, and it encourages others to do the same. Research highlights that it promotes our well-being, facilitates feelings of personal fulfilment, helps tackle societal issues and injustice, and creates a sense of community that transcends the boundaries of countries and states.

✦ PRACTISING GRATITUDE ✦

If we're to protect the world that we share, we need to really *see* all that we have and appreciate it first. Consider the air that you breathe, the streets and paths that you walk along, the wildlife and nature you enjoy. Think about the wonders of modern technology; how a kettle and electricity or gas allows you to make yourself a hot drink with relative ease; the clean water that you can access. Consider personal things such as your loved ones; your ability to think, feel, hear, see, touch, taste smell and speak. Your amazing body allows you to be in this world and seek companionship with others. Allow yourself to feel truly grateful for everything that makes you happy and curious; but remember to forgive yourself when you forget this.

Psychological research tells us that practising gratitude on a daily basis can have a positive effect on our well-being. It can help us to experience a greater sense of contentment and calm, as we recognize what we do have – in spite of life's difficulties – and help us to cope better with the stresses and strains that we'll inevitably face in life.

At a time every day that suits you, see if you can pause and reflect upon what you're grateful for. If you like, write it down in a notebook and take your time. If you notice your mind thinking about what's currently difficult – that's okay. It's normal. See if you can acknowledge the things that you're currently finding hard with compassion, and then make room in your mind for what you are grateful for and glad about, too. Consider these things warmly for a while before you shift the focus of your attention onto something else. Practise this for one week, and reflect upon your experience. What do you notice?

Treating the world with kindness will mean different things to different people, and it can manifest in many different ways; you can make your own choices. Here are some ideas that may prompt or inspire you:

- Try to cultivate your intention to extend kindness to all living beings and the planet, by practising loving-kindness meditations.

- Give to charity; donate things that you no longer need, use or want, rather than throwing them in the bin. It reduces the waste that's piled into landfill sites. Your items might bring someone else a lot of joy.

- On your next birthday, or another special occasion, ask friends and family to donate money to a charity that you care a lot about, instead of buying you gifts.

- Try and travel (responsibly). Get to know other cultures and communities and allow them to open your eyes to all of the different ways of being that exist in this world. Try to understand others with empathy and gain insight into the experiences of minorities.

- You may consider adopting a child (or children) in addition to or instead of reproducing yourself. There are many children in the world in need of a stable loving home; you could give a child a completely different life.

- Start with a genuine smile towards one fellow human being. Kindness begets kindness, creating a better world for us all.

- If you can afford to, sponsor a family in a poorer country to help them overcome generational poverty. Your support could help to meet a family's immediate needs for suitable shelter, food, clean water, education, and employment opportunities.

- Put your phone away sometimes and engage with the human beings that are around you; pay attention to everything that you can see, hear, touch, taste and smell, and allow yourself to feel grateful for it all.

- Many people find strong friendships and support for their issues through social media, and it is a wonderful tool when it's used to help people, truly connect with others, and affect social change. However, research has found that social media usage is also associated with feelings of sadness, jealousy and isolation; it can cause us to crave validation and compare ourselves to others excessively, and it can inhibit our ability to be truly present in the world. Keep this in mind and check in with yourself. Does your social media usage affect your way of being in the world?

- Get active in your local community. Is there anything that you can do to help? Beach cleaning, wildlife protection, volunteering at a homeless shelter or visiting an isolated person through a befriending service?

- Give blood – and/or consider organ donation after your death. Both could save someone's life, or drastically improve it.

- Support independent businesses; visit your local market, bookshop, café, butcher or greengrocer rather than multinational chains.

- Be kind to animals; don't buy products that have directly caused their suffering. For example, fast food that uses intensively farmed animals, or beauty products that've been tested on animals.

If you do buy goods and services from big businesses, research their ethics beforehand and support those who take care of others and the world. Check:

- What's their stance on the use of chemicals in their products?

- Do they recycle?

- Are they transparent about how they do business?

- What's their impact upon the environment?

- Do they offer fair pay, equal rights, fair trade and ethical working conditions?

- Do they take an active, preventative stance on women's rights?

- Do they do good socially?

- Do they endeavour to protect our natural resources with some kind of sustainability strategy? For instance, toilet paper companies that plant trees in an attempt to tackle deforestation.

Be environmentally conscious and reduce your carbon footprint (carbon emissions) whenever possible. For instance, walk or ride a bicycle instead of driving. Become a 'non-buyer' as much as possible. This means acquiring or buying 'pre-loved' items, rather than new things. When less is produced and more is recycled, it's far better for our climate; it promotes sustainability and reduces excessive consumerism.

- Pick up litter – even if it's not yours.

- Avoid buying food and drinks made from non-recyclable materials, and don't use plastic bags (opt for cloth bags instead).

- Endeavour to see our oneness as humans: there's more that we share than what separates us. We all feel fear, anger, disgust, happiness, sadness and surprise. Focus on our fellowship – every face that you see is the same as your mother, father, sister, brother, partner, etc., to someone else. These people are only special to you because you know them and you've formed relationships with them.

- Notice what you're absorbing and try to interact with people who have something kind to say about others. Balance your consumption of challenging news (such as, war, poverty, murder, homophobic and transphobic hate crimes, racism) with stories about human goodness, kindness, aid, support, empathy and compassion. Allow them to uplift you, and share these stories and ideas with others; it positively contributes to the collective ethos.

- Don't underestimate yourself! People like you and I can have great ideas; we can make changes and start movements with the right knowledge and support. Look at the world around you today; what do you see in your local community? Perhaps a communal area in your neighbourhood looks bleak and unloved (for example).

You could get together with some friends, pool the money that you'd spend at the pub in an evening and buy some plants instead. You could clean up the area, plant them together, have fun and watch them bring life to your community. Imagine what we could achieve – what changes we could make, both as individuals and together – if we were a little less self-focused and a little more community-focused.

In our current social, political and economic climate, many of us feel helpless and powerless. Often it is hard to believe that we can do anything to improve things, even on a small scale.

You can

I can

We can

In order to create lasting change, we need to accept the things that we can't control and begin changing the things that we can. Whether it's self-kindness, ways of being kind to others, or kindnesses towards the environment, there are many heart-warming things that we can do that will change us – and this world – for the better.

Where will you begin?

▲▲▲

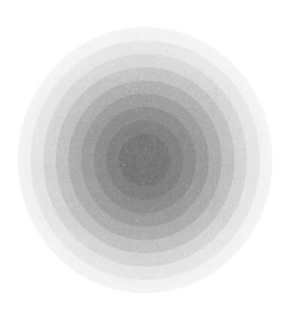

HELPFUL
RESOURCES

HELPFUL RESOURCES

Responding to yourself and others with kindness:

Self-compassion: http://self-compassion.org/

Germer, C. *The Mindful Path to Self-Compassion: Freeing Yourself from Destructive Thoughts and Emotions.* Guilford Press, 2009.

Assertiveness skills training: www.cci.health.wa.gov.au/resources/infopax.cfm?Info_ID=51

Build genuine happiness, and learn how to cope well with life's inevitable challenges:
thehappinesstrap.com

www.imdb.com/title/tt161309/2

Mindfulness resources:

Chödrön, P. *Fail, Fail Again, Fail Better: Wise Advice for Leaning into the Unknown.* Sounds True Inc, 2015.

Chödrön, P. *Taking the Leap: Freeing Ourselves from Old Habits and Fears.* Shambhala Publications Inc, 2010.

Kabat-Zinn, J. *Wherever You Go, There You Are: Mindfulness Meditation in Everyday Life.* Hyperion Books, 1994.

Siegal, D. *Mindsight: Transform Your Brain with the New Science of Kindness.* Oneworld Publications, 2011.

Williams, M., Teasdale, J., Segal, Z., and Kabat-Zinn, J. *The Mindful Way Through Depression: Freeing Yourself From Chronic Unhappiness.* Guilford Press, 2007.

franticworld.com/free-meditations-from-mindfulness/

themindfulnesssummit.com/

www.youtube.com/watch?v=3nwwKbM_vJc

Responding to the world with kindness:

Inspiration: www.thelist.com/52504/small-acts-kindness-changed-world/

www.do-it.org/

www.ditchthelabel.org/campaigns/

Guidance: www.care2.com/greenliving/how-to-evaluate-a-companys-ethical-and-sustainable-impact.html

Awareness: www.storyofstuff.org/movies

ABOUT THE AUTHOR

Dr Sarah Jane Arnold is a Chartered Counselling Psychologist and author. She works in private practice, offering integrative psychological therapy that is tailored to the individual. She supports her clients to understand their pain, break free from limiting vicious cycles, and respond adaptively to difficult thoughts and challenging feelings so that they can live a full and meaningful life.

Sarah lives in Brighton (UK) with her partner Mine, their dog Oprah, and Priscilla the bearded dragon.

You can find Sarah at:
www.themindfulpsychologist.co.uk
www.instagram.com/themindfulpsychologist

▲▲▲

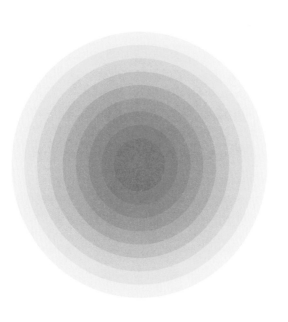